12.95
6/87

JUN 25 '97	DATE DUE		
MAY 17 00			

Animal Habitats

The Butterfly in the Garden

Text by Paul and Mary Whalley

Photographs by
Oxford Scientific Films

Gareth Stevens Publishing
Milwaukee

The Swallowtail is only found in Europe and in a small corner of Britain. In many countries, including Britain, it is protected by law.

The garden butterfly

Butterflies are found in most parts of the world. They occur in the greatest numbers in the tropics, but some are even seen during the short summer north of the Arctic Circle. They are not, however, found south of the Antarctic Circle.

On fine days from spring to autumn, butterflies can be seen in most gardens. They depend a great deal on the warmth of the sun to raise their body temperature and make them active. This is why they fly more on warm sunny days in the cooler parts of the world. In Europe and North America we think of them as part of the summer countryside or yard.

Gardens are different from many wild *habitats*. They have been designed first to please the people who own them, and it is only by accident that they provide food and shelter for so many different wild animals.

Butterflies come into gardens and yards to look for nectar, a sweet, energy-giving liquid found in many flowers. To tempt the butterflies we need to grow fragrant and nectar-rich flowers. Although cultivated roses are beautiful to look at, and even smell sweet, they do not attract butterflies because they have no nectar.

The Red Admiral butterfly is often seen in gardens.

Some butterflies, like the Comma and Small Tortoiseshell, come into our yards in autumn, not just for the flowers, but also to look for a place to spend the winter. These butterflies *hibernate* as adults, hiding during the cold weather in clumps of ivy or in sheds and houses.

Butterflies are insects. They spend the earlier part of their lives as wingless, 16-legged caterpillars and then change into winged, six-legged adults. The caterpillars are often difficult to find. They live in grass, on the underside of leaves, or they are hidden under a silken web on the leaves they eat. But the brightly colored adults are easy to spot as they fly about in the sunshine.

Butterflies use the garden as a first-class restaurant, but they usually have to go out of the garden to find a suitable place to lay their eggs. Unfortunately this is not true of the Cabbage White butterflies, which lay their eggs on our cabbages. When these eggs hatch the caterpillars cause damage to the crops.

One of the few unwelcome garden butterflies is the Cabbage White, whose caterpillars eat the cabbages we grow.

Right: A Swallowtail ready to feed. When it is uncoiled, the proboscis can reach deep into the flower for nectar.

The butterfly's body

Butterflies and moths belong to a group of insects called Lepidoptera, which means "scale-covered." The whole body, apart from the eyes, is covered with scales. These are small and can easily be brushed off. The body of the butterfly is divided into three parts: the head, *thorax*, and *abdomen*.

The main sense *organs* are on the head. Sense organs tell the butterfly what is happening in the world around it. They alert it to dangers and guide it to food and to where other butterflies of its own kind are flying.

The large, rounded eyes are placed on either side of the head. Each one is made up of thousands of little windows or facets. Each facet is like one individual eye, and through them all the insect can build up a picture of the world around it. Butterflies can quickly spot any movement near them. This is important for warning them of danger. Try approaching a butterfly. It may not notice you if you are *very* stealthy but make one rapid movement and it is off! Being able to see in color helps the butterfly to find flowers and also to find and recognize its mate.

The *antennae*, or feelers, stick out from the top of the head. Butterflies wave their antennae around to pick up scents in the air. They can recognize the perfumes from different flowers, and they can also detect the special scents produced by butterflies of the opposite sex. This is very important when they look for a mate. Below the head is a pair of *palps*. These are sense organs which help the butterfly recognize suitable food.

Between the two palps is the *proboscis*, or tongue, a feeding tube. When the insect wants to feed, it uncoils this tube and probes into a flower for nectar in much the same way that we would use a straw to suck the drink out of a bottle. When not in use, the proboscis can be coiled up under the head. Because the proboscis can coil, it can be much longer than if it were carried sticking straight out. Although other insects may have a proboscis, only butterflies and moths can coil theirs up when not in use, so they alone can feed on nectar hidden deeper in the flowers.

The proboscis of this Cabbage White is coiled up under its head.

Here you can see the large rounded eyes and sensitive antennae of the Marbled White butterfly.

The thorax is the powerhouse of the body. Here are attached two pairs of wings and three pairs of legs. The thorax has strong muscles which are used to move the wings and legs. The butterfly's thin, jointed legs are used for walking and for grasping plants. They also have some sense organs for tasting. These are on the tip of the legs: a butterfly can taste through its feet! Many butterflies have three pairs of jointed legs but in some groups, including the Commas, the front legs are very small and are not used for walking.

A Small Tortoiseshell rests with its wings outstretched. You can see that its abdomen is divided into segments.

The wings are the colorful part of the butterfly, and they catch our eyes as the sun strikes them. They are covered with microscopic scales, each one inserted into a small socket on the wing. The scales overlap like the tiles on a roof and are arranged to form the patterns of colors, lines, or spots that we see. Each individual scale has fine ridges along its length. These reflect the light in different ways according to their distance apart and their height. They produce the wonderful colors and metallic sheens which are reflected when the sunlight catches the wing.

The blood of a butterfly is pumped through the body and the wings by the tubular heart and the muscular contractions of the body. In the wings, the blood flows in veins. Inside the body, however, the blood does not run in veins. It bathes the organs.

Both the adult butterfly and the caterpillar need air to breathe. They do not have lungs but take in air through small holes in the side of the body called *spiracles*. The air is passed around the body inside a system of fine tubes.

The abdomen is the long, soft end-part of the body. It contains the digestive system and sex organs.

The wing scales of this Small Tortoiseshell, seen in this close-up, overlap like roof tiles.

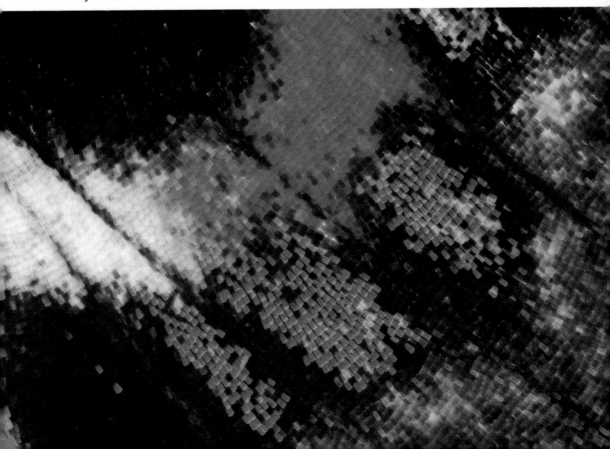

The Monarch flies thousands of miles on migration. Its wingspan can be as much as 4 inches (100mm).

The butterfly's day

Butterflies need the warmth of the sun to make them active. This is why we often see them sitting in the sun with their wings outstretched. Once their bodies are warm, they can fly about. At night, they rest under leaves of plants, waiting for the sun to warm them up again. Each kind of butterfly has its own characteristic flight. The Monarchs and the White Admirals have a slow, lazy, gliding flight, while the small Skipper butterflies have a fast, whirring flight. Some butterflies fly rapidly for a short distance and then stop quickly, closing their wings. They seem to disappear as their *camouflaged* undersides help them to merge into the background. Not surprisingly, butterflies can change their flight patterns if they are chased, and a slow flight can rapidly turn into a zig-zag, darting type.

The outstreched wings of this Small Copper catch the sunlight as it rests on a flower head.

A male Gatekeeper; the name comes from its habit of flying up and down fields and hedges past gates. The female is brighter in color and does not have the dark smudge on its forewing.

Many animals, including butterflies, have a definite *territory* which they regard as their own and defend against others of their kind. Frequently, part or all of a garden may be taken over by one butterfly. Some are very aggressive. A Small Copper not only chases off other male Small Coppers, but also dashes up to chase away other kinds of butterfly from its territory. The Speckled Wood, which loves the shade and speckled sunlight under trees, will defend a small patch of sunlight against other male Speckled Woods. As the sunlight moves, so its territory changes.

In parts of Europe, the Hedge Brown patrols up and down stretches of fields and will often include part of a garden in its territory. This behavior is so typical that the Hedge Brown has another name, Gatekeeper, from its habit of flying up and down fields past the gate.

Commas and Red Admirals in Europe — like the Alfalfa and other butterflies in North America — do not have territories, but they travel far and wide to look for food or a mate. They may turn up anywhere — in yards, parks, or even in the middle of towns.

The dark underside of this Small Tortoiseshell butterfly helps it hide as it roosts under a leaf at night.

The Brimstone's proboscis probes in the flower, seeking the nectar.

Food and feeding

Most butterflies feed on nectar, which is a sweet liquid produced by some flowers. It is rich in sugar and gives butterflies the energy they need to fly. Butterflies find the flowers by scent and sight. They are attracted to the colors and patterns on the petals of many flowers. They probe with their proboscis for the nectar. If you watch them feeding, you can see that they coil and uncoil the proboscis as they look for nectar. Many butterflies visit different flowers, and it is easy to see which ones they prefer in a flower garden. The bramble flower is a great favorite, as are the Michaelmas daisy, alyssum, lavender, ice plant, and, of course, the butterfly bush, buddleia. Butterflies also like many shrubs with attractive flowers, including veronicas, wallflowers, and many others. If you watch butterflies in yards or parks, you will see that they only stop for moments at some flowers; at others, they will settle and uncoil their proboscis. These are flowers that carry nectar and are the ones you could plant in your yard if you would like butterflies to visit it.

While feeding on nectar, butterflies accidentally gather pollen from the flowers onto their heads and carry it to the next flower. This is very important and ensures that the plants become *pollinated*, so that they can produce fruit and seeds to make next year's flowers. Butterflies not only add beauty to a garden — they actually help gardeners.

*A group of Peacocks feeding on buddleia. This plant is
very popular with butterflies and grows well in gardens.*

Some butterflies feed on the sweet liquids produced by greenflies, and they
will also suck up the juices from ripe fruit. Commas and Red Admirals enjoy
feeding on ripe fruit. Some butterflies, like the Purple Emperor, have rather
strange tastes and feed on *carrion*, sucking the liquid from dung or from
rotting animal flesh.

   Butterflies also feed at damp patches of soil, which we believe are rich in
mineral salts. Usually only male butterflies do this, and their behavior is called
"mud puddling." Butterflies will also happily sit on your arm or leg on a hot
dry day and suck up the perspiration, presumably getting some salts from
this. They are quite harmless, and the worst they can do is tickle!

   The female butterfly not only searches for food for herself, but also must
look for the food plant on which to lay her eggs. Most butterflies feed on
different plants from the ones on which they lay their eggs.

The Comma enjoys feeding on overripe fruit as well as nectar.

Courtship and egg-laying

There are four stages in the life cycle of a butterfly, each very different in appearance. Butterflies lay eggs which hatch into caterpillars — small grubs or *larvae* which have no wings. When the caterpillars have grown to their full size, they enter the *chrysalis*, or *pupa*, stage. From each chrysalis an adult butterfly emerges.

The adult butterfly is designed for flight so that it can find a mate and then find the food plant on which the female lays her eggs. In this way the life cycle can continue.

Courtship and mating are the first stages in the life cycle. Male butterflies chase females in flight during courtship. They flutter around and produce a special scent which attracts the female. The female sits on a leaf while the male dances in the air around her. Sometimes they will both flutter upwards, spiralling around as they fly higher and higher. They mate with the tips of their abdomens joined, each partner facing in opposite directions. This has led to stories about two-headed butterflies.

A pair of mating Common Blue butterflies. Although they may fly linked together, tail to tail, they normally stay quietly on plants.

As the Cabbage White female lays each egg, she glues it firmly to the leaf. The eggs are laid in clusters, and all the caterpillars in the group hatch out at about the same time.

After mating, the female butterfly looks for a place to lay her eggs. She will probably have to fly quite far, often out of the garden, to find the right place. Most butterflies are very particular about which plants to lay their eggs on, because this is where the caterpillar will have to feed. The European Comma female looks for a nettle patch on which to lay her eggs. The American Comma lays her eggs on hops, nettles, and certain other plants, while the Common Blue in Europe lays on clovers and other trefoils.

While Commas and Common Blues lay their eggs singly, others, like the Cabbage White, lay eggs in large batches. The caterpillars hatching from these batches stay together and feed in groups. Most butterflies glue their eggs firmly to the plant, but the Marbled White butterfly scatters her eggs in flight. Since the caterpillars feed on grasses, they do not have much trouble finding their food plant.

When the eggs hatch and the baby caterpillars eat their way out through the shell, their first meal is usually the remains of the eggshell!

Butterfly eggs, like this Comma egg, are often patterned and ridged — not smooth like birds' eggs.

As soon as it breaks out of its shell the Comma caterpillar starts to feed.

The caterpillar

The caterpillar's body is divided, like the butterfly's, into segments. It has a head, thorax, and abdomen, but the division between the thorax and the abdomen is not easy to see. The head is different from that of the butterfly. Its antennae are very short, and it has ten or twelve very small eyes arranged in a semicircle of five or six on each side of the head. Below the head is the spinneret, the organ from which the caterpillar spins fine silk.

The caterpillar has three pairs of legs on the thorax. There are usually four pairs of stumpy legs on the middle segments of the abdomen and a pair of claspers at the hind end. Some caterpillars, like the Comma, are tubular and covered in long, branched spines which make them look very hairy. Other caterpillars, like those of the Blue butterflies, are flatter and more slug-like, with only very fine hairs which are difficult to see.

The spines and hairs on this full-grown Comma caterpillar make it unpleasant for any predator to eat.

Caterpillars of the Blue butterflies are slug-like, as this picture of the Holly Blue shows.

The caterpillar is designed as a feeding tube and spends most of its life feeding and growing. It eats different food and feeds in a very different way from the adult butterfly. Its powerful jaws chew up the leaves until only the ribs of the leaf are left. The caterpillars of some kinds of butterfly are *cannibals*, and the larger ones will eat the smaller ones if they meet. Other kinds are *predatory*, and the caterpillars of some of the Blue butterflies feed on the grubs of ants in whose nest they live.

As the caterpillar grows, its skin becomes too tight. Like all insects, it has to shed its skin, or *molt*, to grow bigger. The caterpillar holds onto a plant with its hind claspers and the old skin splits across the back. The caterpillar then crawls out of the old skin. Underneath it has a new, soft skin. Before this can harden, the caterpillar swallows air and stretches itself. It starts to eat again once the new skin has hardened and goes on feeding until eventually it gets too fat for its skin, when it molts again. Caterpillars molt three or four times in their lives.

The Comma caterpillar fixes itself firmly before splitting its skin for the last time.

After the skin has split, the chrysalis is left anchored to the leaf.

Chrysalis to butterfly

Before its final molt (which, in the Comma, is usually the fourth) the caterpillar spins a silken pad on the plant and attaches itself firmly to this by its rear end. This time, when the skin splits, instead of another caterpillar, a smooth, legless chrysalis appears. Some caterpillars, as well as spinning the pad at the base, also spin a slender girdle of silk which holds the chrysalis closer to the plant. Inside the chrysalis the caterpillar slowly changes into an adult butterfly. This change is called *metamorphosis*. The chrysalis does not feed, and, apart from wriggling a bit if touched, it does not move. It looks dead and inactive, but inside there is temendous activity.

After several weeks or months, when all the changes are complete, the chrysalis splits and the butterfly emerges. But not as the handsome creature we see flying — instead it is a damp and crumpled mess! It rests, hanging with its wings down, while the sun warms it and the blood is pumped along the

The colorful wings and large eyes show through the chrysalis as the butterfly forms inside.

The chrysalis has split and the butterfly is beginning to emerge.

After it has fully emerged, the butterfly's crumpled wings straighten and harden before it takes flight. The well-camouflaged underside and tiny "comma" mark from which the Comma gets its name can be seen.

wing veins. This helps to stretch the wings and when they are fully expanded and stiffened, the butterfly is ready to take off. It flies away to feed and find a mate. Once the adult butterfly emerges, it does not grow any more; all its growing took place at the caterpillar stage.

Some butterflies take the whole year or more to grow from egg to adult. Others may take only a couple of months in the warmer weather. These kinds may breed two or three complete generations in one year. In the Comma, the adult of the second *brood*, although it feeds, does not mate, but looks for a place to hibernate for the winter. It finds a quiet corner under evergreen ivy leaves or in a shed or outbuilding. If you find a hibernating butterfly, do not disturb it, as it probably would not survive if you put it outdoors during the winter. Butterflies that hibernate are among the first we see the following spring.

A newly emerged Comma butterfly at a hogweed flower.

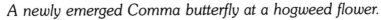

Monarch butterflies resting in clusters at the end of their long migration which takes them from Canada and the northern United States to southern California and Mexico.

Migration

One of the most amazing facts about butterflies is that some of these small, fragile, short-lived insects *migrate* long distances, as birds do. But there are important differences between bird and butterfly migrations.

The migration of butterflies was first noted by the early colonists in North America. The Monarch, a large brown butterfly with a slow, lazy flight, spends the winter in Central America, clinging in millions to the trees. As spring moves north, the Monarchs follow the warmer weather north across the United States and into Canada. In the autumn huge numbers move back southwards towards the southwest United States and Mexico. They could not survive the winter otherwise. They may travel singly, but are more usually seen in large groups or even larger swarms. The main difference between the Monarchs and migratory birds is that the same birds which fly north will return with their young in the autumn. With butterflies, it is usually the next generation that finds its way alone to the south. The Monarch has even been seen in Europe, but it is a rare event, and such butterflies have usually been blown off course.

In Europe butterflies migrate, too, but they are not as spectacular as the Monarchs on migration. Migrants such as the Painted Lady move north every spring from North Africa and the south of France to northern Europe. Many do not make the whole journey. At some point they will stop, mate, and lay eggs, and the butterflies which emerge from this brood will continue the flight north. However, some of the butterflies may fly all the way to northern Europe.

The Cabbage White butterfly, which can survive all the year round in Britain and even further north, is joined each year by new arrivals from the south. In some years Cabbage Whites arrive like clouds. On one occasion a swarm of migrating white butterflies arrived on a cricket field in England in such large numbers that they interrupted the game!

The Red Admirals, Clouded Yellows, and Painted Lady butterflies seen in northern Europe in summer are all migrants which have flown up from the warmer south. They cannot survive over the winter and usually die when the cold weather comes.

The migrant Painted Lady. Look closely, and you will see that the hind wings are slightly damaged. Perhaps it has just completed a long flight.

This Harvest Mouse is feeding on a Small Tortoiseshell.
Butterflies are hunted by many small mammals and birds.

Enemies

A yard surrounded by a hedge or a fence looks like a sheltered place for butterflies, but it also shelters the butterfly's enemies. Plants and flowers attract many kinds of insects, including butterflies, and these insects are important food for small mammals and birds.

The butterfly in the garden has to keep an eye out for enemies. Frogs, toads, lizards, and small mammals, while less able to catch butterflies in flight, are able to stalk them when they are at rest on the ground or on branches.

Many birds try to catch butterflies, and it is common to see a butterfly with a beak mark or a tear in its wing, showing how the butterfly escaped from a hungry bird. Dragonflies will take them in flight, but a greater butterfly killer is the wasp, which pounces on them, nips off their wings, and takes the body back to feed to its grubs. Another hazard for the butterfly in the garden is the spider, which spins its web and waits for butterflies and other insects to fly into it.

The butterfly is in danger from predators at all stages of its life. The eggs are eaten by beetles or lacewings, or the contents may be sucked out by bugs. Snails browsing on the leaves eat any eggs they come across. *Parasitic* wasps lay their eggs inside the eggs of butterflies, and the contents are then eaten by the wasp grubs when they hatch from their eggs. Some of these parasitic wasps lay their eggs in the living caterpillar, which goes on feeding while the parasitic larvae are developing inside it. Eventually the caterpillar is killed by the parasites. Small caterpillars are also at risk from predatory insects like ants, wasps, and lacewing larvae.

A yellow crab spider, hiding on a flower, has caught a butter-fly which landed to feed.

Caterpillars are an important source of food for young birds and other animals like lizards. Birds catch caterpillars by the beakful to feed their young, and it is a common sight to see a Blackbird carrying a load of caterpillars back to its nest.

With all these enemies, it is sometimes a wonder that any butterflies survive! Fortunately, like most insects, butterflies lay many eggs, so, although there are deaths at every stage in the life cycle, some adults survive to breed and start the next generation.

The tiny grubs of a parasitic wasp have emerged from inside this Cabbage White caterpillar.

The Brimstone butterfly looks like a pale green leaf. It uses color and the shape of its wings to disguise itself from predators.

How butterflies protect themselves

Butterflies are showy insects; they are not just hunted for food by birds and other animals, but are also pounced on by playful kittens and other young animals. Unlike bees, they have no sting and no active way of defending themselves. Their first protection is their good eyesight.

The wings are also a means of escape. Once the eyes have alerted the butterfly to danger, it can take off from a plant in a quick, dashing zig-zag. This can save it from small animals on the ground, but it is not always so successful against birds. Sometimes butterflies avoid capture in flight by suddenly dropping to the ground or landing on a leaf and closing their wings. The wings of many butterflies are dull or mottled on the underside. They blend in with their surroundings and make the butterfly difficult to spot. The Comma's ragged wing outline looks like a tattered dead leaf. The Grayling is camouflaged to look like a piece of lichen on the ground or the bark on a tree trunk. At rest with their wings closed, many butterflies lean over towards the sun so that their shadows are made smaller and they are not so easily seen.

Camouflage is not always successful. The Peacock butterfly has another method of survival. It is well camouflaged when its wings are closed, but if an enemy approaches, it quickly flashes open its wings to show four large eyes. These false eyes are round eyespot patterns on the wings. They look like the real eyes of a much bigger animal and frighten away birds and other predators.

The large eyespots on the Peacock butterfly's wings frighten small animals.

Bright colors on the wings, especially red and yellow, usually mean that such butterflies either taste bad or are poisonous. Birds or frogs soon learn that they are not good to eat and in the future leave them alone. A few butterflies, which do not taste bad themselves, copy the patterns of the harmful ones. They therefore escape being eaten by pretending to taste bad. This is called *mimicry*. Swallowtail butterflies and their caterpillars taste bad and are usually avoided by birds.

A butterfly's wings help to protect its body. If a bird pecks at a wing, even if it tears it, the butterfly can escape. If the head or body had been pecked, the butterfly would have been killed. The wings of many butterflies often have spots and patterns which distract the bird from attacking the head or body.

In spite of their many enemies, butterflies have survived longer in the world than humans. Fossil butterflies have been discovered in rocks dating from millions of years before the first human appeared.

In contrast, the undersides of the Peacock's wings are dark and inconspicuous. They blend beautifully with the bark on this tree trunk.

The bright colors of the Monarch caterpillar warn that it tastes nasty.

How the early stages protect themselves

Caterpillars hatching on their food plant do not have to move far for food. This protects them from the watchful eyes of birds which would quickly see movement in the grass. The caterpillars of many Brown butterflies and Skippers, which are grass feeders, feed only at night. At dawn they crawl down the grass stems and hide close to the ground. This not only protects them against daytime predators, but also against grazing animals such as sheep, cattle, and goats which, feeding during the day, would eat them in the grass without noticing.

Caterpillars are most abundant when birds are feeding their young. It is important, therefore, that they have some means of protecting themselves. Brightly colored caterpillars like the Monarch usually taste bad, so, although one or two of a group may be killed, the others are left alone.

Swallowtail caterpillars, like this Australian one, frighten predators by pushing out two long, foul-smelling threads from behind their heads.

Many caterpillars are camouflaged to blend in with their surroundings. Others have hairs or spines which make them prickly and unpleasant to eat. Most, however, rely on being camouflaged and blending in with their background to avoid detection. Swallowtail caterpillars push out two finger-like structures from behind the head when they are attacked. These have a pungent smell; perhaps Swallowtail caterpillars are the skunks of the insect world! Sometimes the caterpillars which feed in groups, like the Pearl Crescent and the Peacock, spin a silken web and live inside it on a leaf, where they are hidden from predators.

Unlike caterpillars, a chrysalis cannot move to escape from predators. It has to be well-hidden or camouflaged to protect itself from enemies. Some are brightly colored and escape enemies by tasting bad.

The chrysalis of this Orange Tip butterfly is hard to spot on the brown stem. At this stage in the life cycle, camouflage is its only defense.

This man is spraying the bank with weedkiller. If we destroy too many weeds we will harm the butterflies, other insects and small animals that feed on them.

Butterflies and humans

People have always admired the patterns and colors of butterflies and wondered about their life history. Paintings of butterflies were found on the tombs of the Kings of ancient Egypt. In Medieval times, monks decorated the pages of their books with sketches of the butterflies they saw in their gardens. Today pictures of butterflies decorate wallpaper, fabrics, and clothes and they are even used in advertisements.

It is a pity that most of the harm done today to these beautiful insects, although unintentional, is caused by humans. One of the most serious threats to butterflies is the destruction of their habitats. Farmers drain marshland to grow crops, and other pieces of land are cleared to build new towns and roads. Butterflies like the Swallowtail and the Large Copper are decreasing in numbers, and marshland butterflies all over the world have disappeared as their wild habitats have been drained. Shrubs and bushes are cut down and the edges of roads cut back or sprayed with weedkiller. This keeps the edges neat and tidy and enables us to move safely along the roads. But when people use sprays to kill insect pests in gardens, parks, and fields, the good and useful insects are also killed. Ladybugs, which eat greenfly, and the bees and butterflies which pollinate flowers are all killed by these *pesticides*.

Fertilizers, too, have a disastrous effect on wild plants, and thus on the animals that feed on them. When a field is treated with fertilizer it usually encourages one or two kinds of plant to grow at the expense of the others, so there is less variety of plants. The numbers of different butterflies will drop, too. The butterflies visiting a garden or yard depend on the surrounding countryside for their survival. If meadows are plowed up and shrubs cut down, then the numbers of butterflies decrease and fewer will find their way into your yard.

Butterflies are the insects we notice more often than others. If they survive, then it is likely that the bees and ladybugs which are also useful will have survived, too. Planning gardens with a lot of flowers, a few wild patches, and the minimum use of chemicals is one of the ways we can help butterflies survive.

After the long winter, we see the first butterfly as a sign of the approach of spring. In Europe the yellow Brimstone is one of the first to appear. The name "butterfly" is believed to come from the Brimstone, whose yellow color reminded people of a "butter-colored fly."

When hedgerows or windbreaks are destroyed and land is burned, as in this picture, butterflies are not the only wildlife to suffer.

Many other insects share the nectar with the butterflies. Here some hoverflies are feeding at a teasel flower.

Friends and neighbors

Butterflies are not the only animals that find gardens and yards attractive places to live. We also see bees, hoverflies, and other insects feeding on the nectar in the flowers. On the stems of roses, lupins, and other plants you may see a mass of greenfly. These in turn attract ladybugs and lacewings, which feed on the greenfly. The butterflies we see feeding on rotting fruit often share this harvest with wasps and other insects. Many insects, both the adults and their larvae, share the plants with caterpillars, which feed on the leaves. Some, like the sawfly larvae, look very similar to caterpillars, but they have more than four pairs of tubular feet in the middle of the body. Crawling around on the ground, under the plants, are beetles, earwigs, and many ants. Slugs and snails which leave slimy trails feed on plants, especially young seedlings, which they share with caterpillars.

If your yard is next to the right kind of field, you may have lizards attracted by a plentiful supply of insects. You do not need to have a pond in your garden or yard to attract frogs and toads. They come in to hunt insects, flicking out their tongues like lightning to catch flies and even butterflies. If you do have a pond, then frogs, toads, and dragonflies will probably stay in your yard.

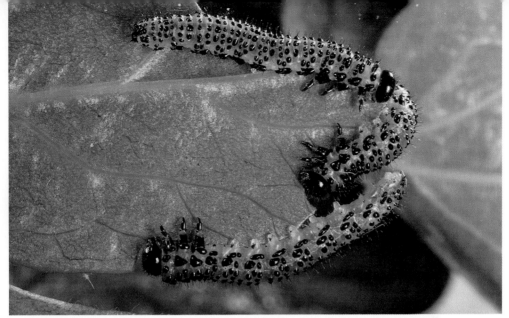

At first glance, this sawfly larva looks like a caterpillar. But is has six pairs of legs in the middle of its body, whereas butterfly caterpillars have only four pairs.

Birds come into the yard at all times of the year. In the spring they need materials like dried grass and broken twigs to build nests; once the eggs have hatched they search for grubs and worms. This is the time of year when they find many caterpillars. Summer is the time when insect-eating birds, like swallows and swifts, dive over the yard catching insects in flight.

Mice and voles find quiet corners and come out mainly at night to feed on seeds and berries, while grey squirrels come to steal nuts and berries and to compete with birds for food on the bird feeder. Other visitors include hedgehogs and foxes, both of which usually come out at night.

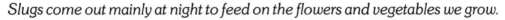

Slugs come out mainly at night to feed on the flowers and vegetables we grow.

Food chain

The animals that visit or live in gardens are all linked together by the food they eat. Although butterflies and their caterpillars feed only on plants, they themselves are the food of other animals in the garden, from wasps to birds. Butterflies and caterpillars are part of a natural food chain in which the energy stored up in the plants is passed through them to the small animals that eat them. These small animals in turn are eaten by larger animals and they, by passing out waste food or by dying, restore the energy to the soil. There, it is taken up by the plants and the cycle begins again.

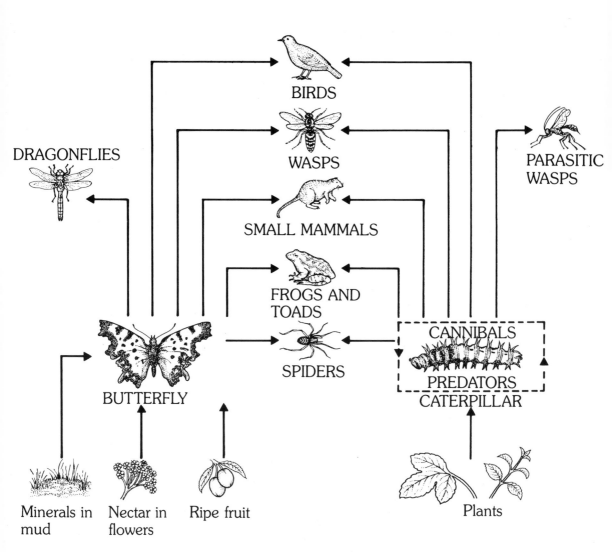

BIRDS

DRAGONFLIES

WASPS

PARASITIC WASPS

SMALL MAMMALS

FROGS AND TOADS

CANNIBALS

BUTTERFLY

SPIDERS

PREDATORS
CATERPILLAR

Minerals in mud

Nectar in flowers

Ripe fruit

Plants

If a space for wild flowers is left in our gardens, we may attract as many butterflies as are found in a meadow like this.

Life in the garden

The changes in modern farming methods and the use of more and more land for building have destroyed many of the traditional breeding places for butterflies. To help butterflies survive, we have to make sure that small corners are left wild and that woodlands and meadows do not completely disappear. Even in our gardens and yards, we can help by leaving a small patch of nettles, or a piece of ground where grasses and wildflowers can grow.

The flowers and shrubs we plant should be colorful and fragrant. We can use the butterfly as a barometer of conditions in the garden. If there are many flying there in the summer, we can be happy about the balance of nature in the garden and know that it is a good place for wildlife.

Glossary

These new words about butterflies appear in the text in *italics*, just as they appear here.

abdomen . . . . . . part of an insect's body behind the thorax

antennae . . . . . . feelers on the butterfly's head; very small on caterpillar's head

brood . . . . young animals; offspring produced at one time

camouflage . . . . animal disguise; the way animals hide by blending with their background

cannibal . . . . an animal which eats its own kind

carrion . . . . dead animals

chrysalis . . . . pupa or resting stage of a butterfly

habitat . . . . the natural home of an animal or plant

hibernate . . . . . . to rest or sleep, often over winter

larvae . . . . caterpillars, grubs, or maggots; plural of *larva*, the young stage of an insect

metamorphosis . change from ground-living caterpillar to flying insect

migration . . . . . . movement of animals at
(migrate) different times of year, usually for breeding or wintering

mimicry . . . . the way in which a harmless animal resembles a poisonous or well-protected animal of the same kind — predators avoid both

molt . . . . to cast off old skin

organ . . . . part of the body with special use, e.g. heart, brain, etc.

palps . . . . feelers; sense organs which help the butterfly find food

parasite . . . . an animal or plant that lives
(parasitic) and feeds on another

pesticides . . . . . . chemicals used to poison insects or other pests

pollination . . . . . the transfer of pollen from
(pollinated) the male to the female parts of a flower

predators . . . . . . animals that kill and eat
(predatory) others

proboscis . . . . . . tubular structure like a drinking straw through which insects suck up liquid food

pupa . . . . the stage in the development of an insect in which the larva changes into an adult

spiracles . . . . holes along the side of an insect's body through which it breathes

territory . . . . piece of land which an animal defends against intruders

thorax . . . . middle part of an insect's body bearing legs and wings

Reading level analysis: SPACHE 3.3, FRY 5, FLESCH 78 (fairly easy), RAYGOR 5-6, FOG 7, SMOG 5.7

Library of Congress Cataloging-in-Publication Data

Whalley, Paul Ernest Sutton. The butterfly in the garden.

(Animal habitats)
Summary: Text and photographs depict butterflies feeding, breeding, and defending themselves in their natural habitats.
1. Butterflies — Juvenile literature. [1. Butterflies] I. Whalley, Mary. II. Oxford Scientific Films. III. Title. IV. Series.
QL544.2.W46 1986   595.78'9   86-5705
ISBN 1-55532-093-7
ISBN 1-55532-068-6 (lib. bdg.)

North American edition first published in 1987 by

Gareth Stevens, Inc. 7221 West Green Tree Road   Milwaukee, WI 53223, USA. Text copyright © 1987 by Oxford Scientific Films. Photographs copyright © 1987 by Oxford Scientific Films.

Typeset by Ries Graphics ltd., Milwaukee. Printed in Hong Kong by South China Printing Co. Series Editor: Jennifer Coldrey. U.S. Editors: MaryLee Knowlton and Mark J. Sachner. Art Director: Treld Bicknell. Design: Naomi Games. Line Drawings: Lorna Turpin. Scientific Consultants: Gwynne Vevers and David Saintsing.

The publishers wish to thank the following for permission to reproduce copyright material: **Oxford Scientific Films Ltd.** for pp. 3 *above*, 6 *above*, 7, 9 *below*, 10, 11 *above*, 12, 13 *below*, 14 *both*, 16 *all*, 17 *both above*, 20, 22, 23 *both*, 28, 29 *below* and back cover (photographer G. I. Bernard); p. 26 and front cover (photographer David Wright); p. 17 *below* and title page (photographer Gordon Maclean); p. 2 (photographer Ian Mear); pp. 3 *below*, 4, 6 *below*, 13 *above*, 21 *below*, 24 and 29 *above* (photographer J. A. L. Cooke); pp. 5, 9 *above* and 25 *below* (photographers J. S. and E. J. Woolmer); pp. 11 *below* and 18 (photographer M. P. L. Fogden); p. 15 (photographer A. C. Allnutt); p. 19 (photographer Peter Parks); p. 21 (photographer Derek Bromhall); p. 25 *above* (photographer D. M. Shale); p. 27 (photographer Raymond Blythe); p. 31 (photographer Paul Whalley); **NHPA**, p. 8 *above* (photographer Stephen Dalton).

32